How to Raise and Train
German Shepherd

By SARA M. BARBARESI

Distributed in the U.S.A. by T.F.H. Publications, Inc., 211 West Sylvania Avenue, P.O. Box 27, Neptune City, N.J. 07753; in England by T.F.H. (Gt. Britain) Ltd., 13 Nutley Lane, Reigate, Surrey; in Canada to the book store and library trade by Clarke, Irwin & Company, Clarwin House, 791 St. Clair Avenue West, Toronto 10, Ontario; in Canada to the pet trade by Rolf C. Hagen Ltd., 3225 Sartelon Street, Montreal 382, Quebec; in Southeast Asia by Y.W. Ong, 9 Lorong 36 Geylang, Singapore 14; in Australia and the south Pacific by Pet Imports Pty. Ltd., P.O. Box 149, Brookvale 2100, N.S.W. Australia. Published by T.F.H. Publications, Inc. Ltd., The British Crown Colony of Hong Kong.

Photos by George Pickow from Three Lions, Inc., taken with the cooperation of Mr. Julius Due, Huntington Station, New York.

ISBN 0-87666-296-3

Library of Congress Catalog Card No. 57-8805

© Copyright, 1957

Contents

A German Shepherd has a healthy appetite. Feed him well but not too much! Don't allow your German Shepherd to grow fat and lazy. Exercise him properly and feed him according to his needs.

1. German Shepherd Standards

The German Shepherd Dog is probably the most international of all breeds. From its original home to Japan and South America, from sheep dog to Rin Tin Tin, the Shepherd lives up to the motto set by the "father of the breed," *Utility and Intelligence.*

That the Shepherd has both, as well as great beauty, is undisputed. He is the most popular family pet and children's companion throughout the world. During the past few years the breed has risen to sixth in American Kennel Club registrations, showing a steady increase in favor. Shepherds make wonderful pets in city apartments as well as country homes and on farms, because they are so easily trained. They have proved their versatility and more than paid their way in many different jobs.

Thousands of Shepherds have served in the armed forces of different countries, and today this is the only breed used by the U.S. services. The first guide dogs for the blind were Shepherds, and the Seeing Eye dogs in this country include more dogs of this breed than all other breeds together.

THE SHEPHERD'S NAME

"German Shepherd Dog" is the complete, correct name for the breed. This is a translation of the German name, established by Capt. Max von Stephanitz who founded the Verein für Deutsche Shäferhunde, S.V. in 1899. In England they are called Alsatians. Although Shepherds are often used as police dogs, "German Police" is not a correct name for the breed.

Another misconception, due to the frequent wolf-gray or tan color and general outline, is that Shepherds are closely related to or descended from the wolf. Of course this is not true. All dogs and dog-like animals, including wolves, foxes, and jackals, descend from a common ancestor, but the breeds of dogs are much more closely related to each other than to any other species, and they have been distinct types for hundreds if not thousands of years. Dogs of the shepherd type were man's first workers, guarding his home and later his flocks and herds—AGAINST wolves and other predators.

The German Shepherd, as a distinct breed selected for certain characteristics of type and temperament, dates from the efforts of von Stephanitz to stabilize and perpetuate the desirable abilities of the working dogs of his day. Attempts to train these dogs for police and war work were made. Several types of herd dogs were used to establish the desired characteristics, including color, gait, size, strength of back, erect ears, and tail carriage.

The German Shepherd Dog Club of America was founded in 1913. Today it is one of the most active and constructive breed clubs in the country, with a large membership, its own magazine, and promotion of many worthwhile causes. Among its early members are the great Shepherd breeders, the late Mr. P. A. B. Widener, who established the breed as THE dog for the Coast Guard; John Gans, who imported the great Pfeffer von Bern and other noted foundation dogs; and Mrs. M. Hartley Dodge of Giralda, Miss Marie Leary of Cosalta, and Lloyd Brackett of Long-Worth.

KENNEL CLUB SPECIFICATIONS

The ideal German Shepherd is a strong, active dog of medium size. It gives an impression of alertness and great litheness and fluidity. The dog lives up to its appearance of greater length than height, and is substantial but not at all clumsy or overweight. Its gait is particularly characteristic, flowing and effortless. The ideal size is 25″ for males and 23″ for females, with weights from 60 to 85 pounds. The coat is double, with a harsh outer coat and softer protective under coat. Colors go all the way from black through black-and-tan or black-and-silver to cream. Rich colors are generally preferable to faded ones, and white is undesirable, as evidence of weakness.

Here are the standards by which the Shepherd is judged, drawn up by the German Shepherd Dog Club of America, and approved by the Board of Directors of the American Kennel Club:

GENERAL APPEARANCE: The first impression of a good German Shepherd Dog is that of a strong, agile, well-muscled animal, alert and full of life. It should both be and appear to be well-balanced, with harmonious development of the forequarter and hindquarter. The dog should appear to the eye, and actually be, longer than tall; deep-bodied, and presenting an outline of smooth curves rather than corners. It should look substantial and not spindly, giving the impression, both at rest and in motion, of muscular fitness and nimbleness without any look of clumsiness or soft living.

The ideal height for dogs is 25 inches, and for bitches, 23 inches at the shoulder. This height is established by taking a perpendicular line from the top of the shoulder blade to the ground with the coat parted or so pushed down that this measurement will show only the actual height of the frame or structure of the dog. The working value of dogs above or below the indicated heights is proportionately lessened, although variations of an inch above or below the ideal height are acceptable, while greater variations must be considered as faults. Weights of dogs of desirable size in proper flesh and condition average between 75 and 85 pounds, and of bitches, between 60 and 70 pounds.

The Shepherd should be stamped with a look of quality and nobility—difficult to define but unmistakable when present. The good Shepherd Dog never looks common.

The familiar, magnificent stance of a German Shepherd is completely, dynamically balanced. At rest as well as in motion, he is the picture of alertness.

The breed has a distinct personality marked by a direct and fearless, but not hostile, expression; self-confidence and a certain aloofness which does not lend itself to immediate and indiscriminate friendships.

Secondary sex characteristics should be strongly marked, and every animal should give a definite impression of masculinity or femininity, according to its sex. Dogs should be definitely masculine in appearance and deportment; bitches, unmistakably feminine, without weakness of structure or apparent softness of temperament.

Male dogs having one or both testicles undescended (monorchids or cryptorchids) are to be disqualified.

The condition of the dog should be that of an athlete in good condition, the muscles and flesh firm and the coat lustrous.

The Shepherd is normally a dog with a double coat, the amount of undercoat varying with the season of the year and the proportion of the time the dog spends out of doors. It should, however, always be present to a sufficient degree to keep out water, to insulate against temperature

The intelligent look of a German Shepherd makes you think he's almost human. Nobility characterizes his clean-cut features.

extremes, and as a protection against insects. The outer coat should be as dense as possible, hair straight, harsh and lying close to the body. A slightly wavy outer coat, often of wiry texture, is equally permissible. The head, including the inner ear, foreface and legs and paws are covered with short hair, and the neck with longer and thicker hair. The rear of forelegs and hind legs has somewhat longer hair extending to the pastern and hock respectively. Faults in coat include complete lack of any undercoat, soft, silky or too long outer coat and curly or open coat.

STRUCTURE: A German Shepherd is a trotting dog and his structure has been developed to best meet the requirements of his work in herding. That is to say, a long, effortless trot which shall cover the maximum amount of ground with the minimum number of steps, consistent with the size of the animal. The proper body proportion, firmness of back and muscles and the proper angulation of the forequarters and hindquarters serve this end. They enable the dog to propel itself forward by a long step of the hindquarter and to compensate for this stride by a long step of the forequarter. The high withers, the firm back, the strong loin, the properly formed croup, even the tail as balance and rudder, all contribute to this same end.

PROPORTION: The German Shepherd Dog is properly longer than tall with the most desirable proportion as 10 is to 8½. We have seen how the height is ascertained; the length is established by a dog standing naturally and four-square, measured on a horizontal line from the point of the prosternum, or breastbone, to the rear edge of the pelvis, the ischium tuberosity, commonly called the sitting bone.

ANGULATION: (a) FOREQUARTER: The shoulder blade should be long, laid on flat against the body with its rounded upper end in a vertical line above the elbow, and sloping well forward to the point where it joins the upper arm. The withers should be high, with shoulder blades meeting closely at the top, and the upper arm set on at an angle approaching as nearly as possible a right angle. Such an angulation permits the maximum forward extension of the foreleg without binding or effort. Shoulder faults include too steep or straight a position of either blade or upper arm, too short a blade or upper arm, lack of sufficient angle between these two members, looseness through lack of firm ligamentation, and loaded shoulders with prominent pads of flesh or muscles on the outer side. Construction in which the whole shoulder assembly is pushed too far forward also restricts the stride and is faulty.

(b) HINDQUARTERS: The angulation of the hindquarter also consists ideally of a series of sharp angles as far as the relation of the bones to each other is concerned, and the thigh bone should parallel the shoulder blade while the stifle bone parallels the upper arm. The whole assembly of the thigh, viewed from the side, should be broad, with both thigh and stifle well muscled and of proportionate length, forming as nearly as possible a right angle. The metacarpus (the unit between the hock joint and the foot commonly and erroneously called the hock) is strong, clean and short, the hock joint clean-cut and sharply defined.

HEAD: Clean-cut and strong, the head of the Shepherd is characterized by nobility. It should seem in proportion to the body and should not be clumsy, although a degree of coarseness of head, especially in dogs, is less of a fault than overrefinement. A round or domey skull is a fault. The muzzle is long and strong with the lips firmly fitted, and its top line is usually parallel with an imaginary elongation of the line of the forehead. Seen from the front, the forehead is only moderately arched and the skull slopes into the long wedge-shaped muzzle without abrupt stop. Jaws are strongly developed. Weak and too narrow underjaws, snipey muzzles and no stop are faults.

(a) EARS: The ears should be moderately pointed, open toward the front, and are carried erect when at attention, the ideal carriage being one in which the center lines of the ears, viewed from the front, are parallel to each other and perpendicular to the ground. Puppies usually do not permanently raise their ears until the fourth or sixth month, and sometimes not until later. Cropped and hanging ears are to be discarded. The well-placed and well-carried ear of a size in proportion to the skull materially adds to the general appearance of the Shepherd. Neither too large nor too small ears are desirable. Too much stress, however, should not be laid on perfection of carriage if the ears are fully erect.

(b) EYES: Of medium size, almond-shaped, set a little obliquely and not protruding. The color as dark as possible. Eyes of lighter color are sometimes found and are not a serious fault if they harmonize with the general coloration, but a dark brown eye is always to be preferred. The expression should be keen, intelligent and composed.

(c) TEETH: The strong teeth, 42 in number—20 upper and 22 lower —are strongly developed and meet in a scissor grip in which part of the inner surface of the upper teeth meets and engages part of the outer surface of the lower teeth. This type of bite gives a more powerful grip than one in which the edges of the teeth meet directly, and is subject to less wear. The dog is overshot when the lower teeth fail to engage the inner surfaces of the upper teeth. This is a serious fault. The reverse condition—an undershot jaw—is a very serious fault. While missing premolars are frequently observed, complete dentition is decidedly to be preferred. So-called distemper teeth and discolored teeth are faults whose seriousness varies with the degree of departure from the desired white, sound coloring. Teeth broken by accident should not be severely penalized but worn teeth, especially the incisors, are often indicative of the lack of a proper scissor bite, although some allowance should be made for age.

NECK: The neck is strong and muscular, clean-cut and relatively long, proportionate in size to the head and without loose folds of skin. When the dog is at attention or excited, the head is raised and the neck carried high, otherwise typical carriage of the head is forward rather than up and but little higher than the top of the shoulder, particularly in motion.

TOP LINE: (a) WITHERS: The withers should be higher than, and sloping into, the level back to enable a proper attachment of the shoulder blades.

(b) BACK: The back should be straight and very strongly developed without sag or roach, the section from the wither to the croup being rela-

The German Shepherd is often called a "police dog." His alert appearance and sense of responsibility as well as his work with the armed services and law-enforcement departments have earned him that respected name.

tively short. (The desirable long proportion of the Shepherd Dog is not derived from a long back but from over-all length with relation to height, which is achieved by breadth of forequarter and hindquarter viewed from the side.)

(c) LOIN: Viewed from the top, broad and strong, blending smoothly into the back without undue length between the last rib and the thigh, when viewed from the side.

(d) CROUP: Should be long and gradually sloping. Too level or flat a croup prevents proper functioning of the hindquarter, which must be able to reach well under the body. A steep croup also limits the action of the hindquarter.

(e) TAIL: Bushy, with the last vertebra extended at least to the hock joint, and usually below. Set smoothly into the croup and low rather than high, at rest the tail hangs in a slight curve like a sabre. A slight hook—sometimes carried to one side—is faulty only to the extent that it mars general appearance. When the dog is excited or in motion, the curve is accentuated and the tail raised, but it should never be lifted beyond a line at right angles with the line of the back. Docked tails, or those which have been operated upon to prevent curling, disqualify. Tails too short, or with clumpy ends due to the ankylosis or growing together of the vertebrae, are serious faults.

BODY: The whole structure of the body gives an impression of depth and solidity without bulkiness.

(a) FORECHEST: Commencing at the prosternum, should be well-filled and carried well down between the legs with no sense of hollowness.

(b) CHEST: Deep and capacious with ample room for lungs and heart. Well carried forward, with the prosternum, or process of the breastbone, showing ahead of the shoulder when the dog is viewed from the side.

(c) RIBS: Should be well sprung and long, neither barrel-shaped nor too flat, and carried down to a breastbone which reaches to the elbow. Correct ribbing allows the elbow to move back freely when the dog is at a trot, while too round a rib causes interference and throws the elbow out. Ribbing should be carried well back so that loin and flank are relatively short.

(d) ABDOMEN: Firmly held and not paunchy. The bottom line of the Shepherd is only moderately tucked up in flank, never like that of a Greyhound.

LEGS: (a) The bone of the legs should be straight, oval rather than round or flat and free from sponginess. Its development should be in proportion to the size of the dog and contribute to the over-all impression of substance without grossness. Crooked leg bones and any malformation such as, for example, that caused by rickets, should be penalized.

(b) PASTERN: Should be of medium length, strong and springy. Much more spring of pastern is desirable in the Shepherd Dog than in many other breeds, as it contributes to the ease and elasticity of the trotting gait. The upright terrier pastern is definitely undesirable.

(c) METACARPUS (the so-called "hock"): Short, clean, sharply defined and of great strength. This is the fulcrum upon which much of the forward movement of the dog depends. Cowhocks are a decided fault, but before penalizing for cowhocks, it should be definitely determined, with the animal in motion, that the dog has this fault, since many dogs with exceptionally good hindquarter angulation occasionally stand so as to give the appearance of cowhockedness which is not actually present.

(d) FEET: Rather short, compact, with toes well-arched, pads thick and hard, nails short and strong. The feet are important to the working qualities of the dog. The ideal foot is extremely strong with good gripping power and plenty of depth of pad. The so-called cat-foot, or terrier foot is not desirable. The thin, spread or hare-foot is, however, still more undesirable.

PIGMENT: The German Shepherd Dog differs widely in color and all colors are permissible. Generally speaking, strong, rich colors are to be preferred, with definite pigmentation and without the appearance of washed-out color. White dogs are not desirable and are to be disqualified if showing albino characteristics.

GAIT: (a) General impression: The gait of the German Shepherd Dog is outreaching, elastic, seemingly without effort, smooth and rhythmic. At a walk it covers a great deal of ground, with long step of both hind leg and foreleg. At a trot, the dog covers still more ground and moves powerfully but easily with a beautiful co-ordination of back and limbs so that, in the best examples, the gait appears to be the steady motion of a well-lubricated machine. The feet travel close to the ground, and neither fore nor hind feet should lift high on either forward reach or backward push.

(b) The hindquarter delivers, through the back, a powerful forward thrust which slightly lifts the whole animal and drives the body forward. Reaching far under, and passing the imprint left by the front foot, the strong arched hind foot takes hold of the ground; then hock, stifle and upper thigh come into play and sweep back, the stroke of the hind leg finishing with the foot still close to the ground in a smooth follow-through. The over-reach of the hindquarter usually necessitates one hind foot passing outside and the other hind foot passing inside the track of the forefeet and such action is not faulty unless the locomotion is crabwise with the dog's body sideways out of the normal straight line.

(c) In order to achieve ideal movement of this kind, there must be full muscular co-ordination throughout the structure with the action of muscles and ligaments positive, regular and accurate.

(d) Back transmission: The typical smooth, flowing gait of the Shepherd Dog cannot be maintained without great strength and firmness (which does not mean stiffness) of back. The whole effort of the hindquarter is transmitted to the forequarter through the muscular and bony structure of the loin, back and withers. At full trot, the back must remain firm and level without sway, roll, whip or roach.

(e) To compensate for the forward motion imparted by the hindquarter, the shoulder should open to its full extent—the desirability of good shoulder angulation now becomes apparent—and the forelegs should reach out in a stride balancing that of the hindquarter. A steep shoulder will cause the dog either to stumble or to raise the forelegs very high in an effort to co-ordinate with the hindquarter, which is impossible when shoulder structure is faulty. A serious gait fault results when a dog moves too low in front, presenting an unlevel top line with the wither lower than the hips.

(f) The Shepherd Dog does not track on widely separated parallel lines as does the terrier, but brings the feet inward toward the middle line of the body when at trot in order to maintain balance. For this reason a dog viewed from the front or rear when in motion will often seem to travel close. This is not a fault if the feet do not strike or cross, or if the knees or shoulders are not thrown out, but the feet and hocks should be parallel even if close together.

(g) The excellence of gait must also be evaluated by viewing from the side the effortless, properly co-ordinated covering of ground.

CHARACTER: As has been noted before, the Shepherd Dog is not one that fawns upon every new acquaintance. At the same time, it should be approachable, quietly standing its ground and showing confidence and a willingness to meet overtures without itself making them. It should be poised, but when the occasion demands, eager and alert; both fit and willing to serve in any capacity as companion, watch dog, blind leader, herding dog or guardian, whichever the circumstances may demand.

The Shepherd Dog must not be timid, shrinking behind its master or handler; nervous, looking about or upward with anxious expression or showing nervous reactions to strange sounds or sights, nor lackadaisical, sluggish or manifestly distinterested in what goes on about him. Lack of confidence under any surroundings is not typical of good character; cases of extreme timidity and nervous unbalance sometimes give the dog an apparent, but totally unreal, courage and it becomes a "fear biter," snapping not for any justifiable reason but because it is apprehensive of the approach of a stranger. This is a serious fault subject to heavy penalty.

In Summary: It should never be forgotten that the ideal Shepherd is a working animal, which must have an incorruptible character combined with body and gait suitable for the arduous work which constitutes its primary purpose. All its qualities should be weighed in respect to their contribution to such work, and while no compromise should be permitted with regard to its working potentiality, the dog must nevertheless possess a high degree of beauty and nobility.

Evaluation of Faults—Note: Faults are important in the order of their group, as per group headings, irrespective of their position in each group.

German Shepherds love children and they get along with them very well. They make excellent pets, and in households with children they can serve as outdoor baby-sitters.

Disqualifying Faults—Albino characteristics; cropped ears; hanging ears (as in a hound); docked tails; monorchidism; cryptorchidism.

Very Serious Faults—Major faults of temperament; undershot lower jaw.

Serious Faults—Faults of balance and proportion; poor gait, viewed either from front, rear or side; marked deficiency of substance (bone or body); bitchy male dogs; faulty backs; too level or too short croup; long and weak loin; very bad feet; ring tails; tails much too short; rickety condition; more than four missing premolars or any other missing teeth, unless due to accident; lack of nobility; badly washed-out color; badly overshot bite.

Faults—Doggy bitches; poorly carried ears; too fine heads; weak muzzles; improper muscular condition; faulty coat, other than temporary condition; badly affected teeth.

Minor Faults—Too coarse heads; hooked tails; too light, round or protruding eyes; discolored teeth; condition of coat, due to season or keeping.

DISQUALIFICATIONS: White if indicative of albino characteristics. Cropped ears, hanging ears. Docked tail. Monorchidism, cryptorchidism.

2. Buying Your German Shepherd

Once you have decided that you want a German Shepherd, the next thing is to go about getting him. Perhaps you chose a Shepherd because a neighbor's dog had puppies and the children talked you into it. If the puppies are for sale, your task is an easy one. But more likely you just decided that the German Shepherd was the dog for you and now you have to find the right one.

First, make up your mind what you want: male or female, adult or puppy, show dog or "just a pet." There is no greater use for a dog than being "just" a beloved pet and companion, but the dog which has profitable show and breeding possibilities is worth more to the seller.

PET OR SHOW DOG?

The puppy with a slight flaw in the fit of his teeth or curve of his legs will make just as good a companion and guardian, but his more perfect litter mate will cost more.

That is why there is often a difference in price between puppies which look—to you, anyway—identical. If you think you may want to show your dog or raise a litter of puppies for the fun of it later on, by all means buy the best you can afford. You will save expense and disappointment later on. However, if the puppy is *strictly* a pet for the children, or companion for you, you can afford to look for a bargain. The pup which is not show material; the older pup, for which there is often less demand; or the grown dog, not up to being used for breeding, are occasionally available and are opportunities to save money. Remember that these are the only real bargains in buying a dog. It takes good food and care—and plenty of both—to raise a healthy, vigorous puppy.

The price you pay for your dog is little compared to the love and devotion he will return over the many years he'll be with you. With good care and affection your pup should live to a ripe old age; through modern veterinary science and nutrition, dogs are better cared for and living longer. Their average life expectancy is now eight or nine years, and dogs in their teens are not uncommon.

You can always tell the size to which a puppy will grow by the relative size of its feet to the rest of its body. A good German Shepherd puppy will have heavy paws.

MALE OR FEMALE?

If you should intend breeding your dog in the future, by all means buy a female. You can find a suitable mate without difficulty when the time comes, and have the pleasure of raising a litter of pups—there is nothing cuter than a fat, playful puppy. If you don't want to raise puppies, your female can be spayed, and will remain a healthy, lively pet. The female is smaller than the male and generally quieter. She has less tendency to roam

Before your children handle the puppies, teach them their responsibilities toward all animals: to treat them with care and kindness.

in search of romance, but a properly trained male can be a charming pⁱ and has a certain difference in temperament that is appealing to many people. Male vs. female is chiefly a matter of personal choice.

ADULT OR PUP?

Whether to buy a grown dog or a small puppy is another question. It is undeniably fun to watch your dog grow all the way from a baby, sprawling and playful, to a mature, dignified dog. If you don't have the time to spend on the more frequent meals, housebreaking, and other training a puppy needs in order to become a dog you can be proud of, then choose an older, partly trained pup or a grown dog. If you want a show dog, remember that no one, not even an expert, can predict with 100% accuracy what a small puppy will be when he grows up. He may be right *most* of the time, but six months is the earliest age for the would-be exhibitor to pick a prospect and know that his future is relatively safe.

If you have a small child it is best to get a puppy big enough to defend himself, one not less than four or five months old. Older children will enjoy playing with and helping to take care of a baby pup, but at less than four months a puppy wants to do little but eat and sleep, and he must be protected from teasing and overtiring. You cannot expect a very young child to understand that a puppy is a fragile living being; to the youngster he is a toy like his stuffed dog.

WHERE TO BUY

You can choose among several places to buy your dog. One is a kennel which breeds show dogs as a business and has extra pups for sale as pets. Another is the one-dog owner who wants to sell the puppies from an occasional litter, paying for the expenses being his chief aim. Pet shops usually buy puppies from overstocked kennels or part-time hobbyists for re-sale, and you can generally buy a puppy there at a reasonable price. To find any of these, watch the pet column of your local newspaper or look in the classified section of your phone book. If you or your friends go driving out in the countryside, be on the lookout for a sign announcing pure-bred puppies for sale.

Whichever source you try, you can usually tell in a very short time whether the puppies will make healthy and happy pets. If they are clean, fat and lively, they are probably in good health. At the breeder's you will have the advantage of seeing the puppies' mother and perhaps the father and other relatives. Remember that the mother, having just raised a demanding family, won't be looking her best, but if she is sturdy, friendly and well-mannered, her puppies should be, too. If you feel that something is lacking in the care or condition of the dogs, it is better to look elsewhere than to buy hastily and regret it afterward.

You may be impatient to bring home your new dog, but a few days will make little difference in his life with you. Often it is a good idea to choose a puppy and put a deposit on him, but wait to take him home until you have prepared for the new arrival. For instance, it is better for the Christmas puppy to be settled in his new home before the holidays, or else to wait until things have settled down afterward. You may want to wait until the puppy has completed his "shots," and if this is arranged in advance, it is generally agreeable.

If you cannot find the dog you want locally, write to the secretary of the A.K.C. (page 21), for names of breeders near you, or to whom you can write for information. Puppies are often bought by mail from reputable breeders.

These healthy little fellows have made themselves comfortable already. They are just as happy snuggled up to a human as they are to their mother . . . except when they get hungry.

WHAT TO LOOK FOR IN A PUPPY

In choosing your puppy, assuming that it comes from healthy, well-bred parents, look for one that is friendly and out-going. The biggest pup in the litter is apt to be somewhat coarse as a grown dog, while the appealing "poor little runt" may turn out to be a timid shadow—or have a Napoleon complex! If you want a show dog and have no experience in choosing the prospect, study the standard (page 6), but be advised by the breeder on the finer points of conformation. His prices will be in accord with the puppies' expected worth, and he will be honest with you because it is to his own advantage. He wants his good puppies placed in the public eye to reflect glory on him—and to attract future buyers.

The puppy should have a bright eye, dark in color, giving a keen expression. The head should be long and clean-cut rather than blocky, although the puppy is heavier in proportion than the adult. The stop, or break, between planes of skull and foreface should be pronounced and the jaw strong with teeth meeting in a scissors bite—upper teeth overlapping lower. The ears should give promise of standing erect after teething, as "hound ears" are a disqualifying fault, but they often flop, off and on, while the puppy is growing. The body should be deep and rather long in proportion to height. For the grown dog to have sufficient substance, the puppy's bone must seem disproportionately large, with feet to match. Due to the great length and reach of stride, the puppy will normally stand with hind legs slightly behind, or one behind and one under his body. To provide the thrust demanded in gait, the German Shepherd has extreme angulation, that is, the bones of the hindquarters meet at as near right angles as possible, and the forequarter corresponds. The puppy will not move with the easy grace of the mature dog, but he should show the reach and strength in potential. The tail should be long and sweeping.

Now that you have paid your money and made your choice, you are ready to depart with puppy, papers and instructions. Make sure that you know his feeding routine, and take along some of the food. It is best to make any diet changes gradually so as not to upset his digestion. If the puppy is not fed before leaving he will ride comfortably on your lap where he can see out of the window. Take along a rag or newspapers for accidents.

PEDIGREES

When you buy your puppy you should receive his pedigree and registration certificate or application. These have nothing to do with licensing, which is a local regulation applying to pure-bred and mongrel alike. Find out the local ordinance in regard to age, etc., buy a license, and keep it on your dog whenever he is off your property.

Your dog's pedigree is a chart, for your information only, showing his ancestry. It is not part of his official papers. The registration certificate is the important part. If the dog was named and registered by his breeders you will want to complete the transfer and send it, with the fee of $1.00, to the American Kennel Club, 221 Fourth Ave., New York 3, N. Y. They will transfer the dog to your ownership in their records, and send a new certificate to you.

If you receive instead, an application for registration, you should fill it out, choosing a name for your pup, and mail it with the fee of $2.00 to the A.K.C. Be sure that the number of the puppy's litter is included.

3. Care of the
German Shepherd Puppy

BRINGING YOUR PUPPY HOME

When you bring your puppy home, remember that he is used to the peace and relative calm of a life of sleeping, eating and playing with his brothers and sisters. The trip away from all this is an adventure in itself, and so is adapting to a new home. So let him take it easy for awhile. Don't let the whole neighborhood pat and poke him at one time. Be particularly careful when children want to handle him, for they cannot understand the difference between a delicate living puppy and the toy dog they play with and maul. If the puppy is to grow up loving children and taking care of them, he must not get a bad first impression.

THE PUPPY'S BED

It is up to you to decide where the puppy will sleep. Unless it is winter in a cold climate, even a young puppy can sleep outside in a snug, well-built dog house. It should have a tight, pitched roof to let the rain run off, and a floor off the ground, to avoid dampness. The door should be no larger than the grown dog will need to go in and out, as a bigger opening lets in too much draft. For bedding you can use an old rag or blanket, straw, or sweet-smelling cedar shavings. Whether the puppy sleeps indoors or out, he will benefit from an outdoor run of his own where he can be put to exercise and amuse himself. It does not have to be large for if he goes for walks and plays with you he will get enough exercise that way. He is much safer shut in his run than being left loose to follow a stray dog off your property and get into bad habits—if he isn't hit by a car first!

Of course if the dog is left in his run for any length of time he should have protection from the cold, rain or sun. The run should be rectangular, and as big as you can conveniently make it up to 20 feet x 40 feet, with strong wire fence which will keep your dog in and intruders out. The wire should be at least four feet high, as many dogs like to jump, and the gate should be fastened with a spring hook or hasp which is not likely to be unfastened by mischance.

If your dog sleeps indoors, he should have his own place, and not be allowed to climb all over the furniture. He should sleep out of drafts, but

Feed your German Shepherd puppies in a dish large enough to enable each of them to get his own little ration. Newspapers under the dish will protect the floor from these playful creatures. Note the little pup in the middle sitting right on top of the food so that brothers and sisters can't get at the chow!

not right next to the heat, which would make him too sensitive to the cold when he goes outside. If your youngster wants him to sleep on his bed, that is all right, too, but the puppy must learn the difference between his bed and other furniture. He may sleep on a dog bed or in a box big enough to curl up in: a regulation dog crate or one made from a packing box, with bedding for comfort. If your cellar is dry and fairly warm the puppy will be all right there, or in the garage.

You have already decided where the puppy will sleep before you bring him home. Let him stay there, or in the corner he will soon learn is "his," most of the time, so that he will gain a sense of security from the familiar. Give the puppy a little milk with bread or kibble in it when he arrives, but don't worry if he isn't hungry at first. He will soon develop an appetite when he grows accustomed to his surroundings. The first night the puppy may cry a bit from lonesomeness, but if he has an old blanket or rug to curl up in he will be cozy. In winter a hot water bottle will help replace the warmth of his littermates, or the ticking of a clock may provide company.

FEEDING YOUR PUPPY

It is best to use the feeding schedule to which the puppy is accustomed, and stick to it except when you feel you can modify or improve it. You will probably want to feed the puppy on one of the commercially prepared dog foods as a base, flavoring it with table scraps and probably a little meat and fat when you have them. Remember that the dog food companies have prepared their food so that it is a balanced ration in itself, and, indeed, many dogs are raised on dog food alone. If you try to change this balance too much you are likely to upset your pet's digestion, and the dog will not be as well fed in the long run. Either kibble or meal is a good basic food, and the most economical way to feed your dog.

Milk is good for puppies and some grown dogs like it. Big bones are fine to chew on, especially for teething puppies, but small bones such as chicken, chop or fish bones are always dangerous; they may splinter or stick in the digestive tract. Table scraps such as meat, fat, or vegetables will furnish variety and vitamins, but fried or starchy foods such as potatoes and beans will not be of much food value. Adding a tablespoonful of fat (lard or drippings) to the daily food will keep your puppy's skin healthy and make his coat shine.

Remember that all dogs are individuals. It is the amount that will keep your dog in good health which is right for him, not the "rule-book" amount. A feeding chart to give you some idea of what the average puppy will eat follows:

WEANING TO 3 MONTHS: *A.M.* 1 cup dog food; mixed with warm water. *Noon* 1 cup milk; cereal, kibble, or biscuits. *P.M.* ½ cup dog food; ¼ lb. meat; 1 tbs. fat, scraps. *Bedtime* 1 cup milk; biscuit.

3—6 MONTHS: *A.M.* 2 cups dog meal or kibble, mixed. *Noon* 1 cup milk; soft-boiled egg twice a week. *P.M.* 1 cup meal, as above.

6 MONTHS—1 YEAR: *A.M.* 3 cups of dog meal; or milk with kibble. *P.M.* 2 cups of meal with ½ lb. meat, fat, scraps.

OVER 1 YEAR: *A.M.* half of evening meal if you prefer. *P.M.* 4-5 cups meal, as above.

You can try a system of self-feeding instead of giving your puppy regular meals. This means keeping the dry meal or kibble in front of him all the time. If he is inclined to overeat, put out only the daily amount each morning. Otherwise you can leave a filled dish or pail (protected from the weather and insects if outside) where he can nibble at leisure.

HOUSEBREAKING YOUR PUPPY

As soon as you get your puppy you can begin to housebreak him but remember that you can't expect too much of him until he is five months old or so. A baby puppy just cannot control himself, so it is best to give him an opportunity to relieve himself before the need arises.

Don't let the puppy wander through the whole house; keep him in one or two rooms under your watchful eye. If he sleeps in the house and has been brought up on newspapers, keep a couple of pages handy on the floor. When he starts to whimper, puts his nose to the ground or runs around looking restless, take him to the paper before an "accident" occurs. After he has behaved, praise him and let him roam again. It is much better to teach him the right way than to punish him for misbehaving. Puppies are naturally clean and can be housebroken easily, given the chance. If a mistake should occur, and mistakes are bound to happen, wash it immediately with tepid water, followed by another rinse with water to which a few drops of vinegar have been added. A dog will return to the same place if there is any odor left, so it is important to remove all traces.

If your puppy sleeps outside, housebreaking will be even easier. Remember that the puppy has to relieve himself after meals and whenever he

Train your puppy as early as possible to relieve himself on the paper unless you are able to take him outside every few hours. He'll be quick to learn what's expected of him.

wakes up, as well as sometimes in between. So take him outside as soon as he shows signs of restlessness indoors, and stay with him until he has per-formed. Then praise and pat him, and bring him back inside as a reward. Since he is used to taking care of himself outdoors, he will not want to misbehave in the house, and will soon let you know when he wants to go out.

You can combine indoor paper training and outdoor housebreaking by taking the puppy out when convenient and keeping newspaper available for use at other times. As the puppy grows older he will be able to control himself for longer periods. If he starts to misbehave in the house, without asking to go out first, scold him and take him out or to his paper. Punish-ment *after* the fact will accomplish nothing; the puppy cannot understand why he is being scolded unless it is immediate.

The older puppy or grown dog should be able to remain overnight in the house without needing to go out, unless he is ill. If your dog barks or acts restless, take him out once, but unless he relieves himself right away, take him back indoors and shut him in his quarters. No dog will soil his bed if he can avoid it, and your pet will learn to control himself overnight if he has to.

THE FEMALE PUPPY

If you want to spay your female you can have it done while she is still a puppy. Her first seasonal period will probably occur between eight and ten months, although it may be as early as six or delayed until she is a year old. She may be spayed before or after this, or you may breed her (at a later season) and still spay her afterward.

The first sign of the female's being in season is a thin red discharge, which will increase for about a week, when it changes color to a thin yellowish stain, lasting about another week. Simultaneously there is a swell-ing of the vulva, the dog's external sexual organ. The second week is the crucial period, when she could be bred if you wanted her to have puppies, but it is possible for the period to be shorter or longer, so it is best not to take unnecessary risks at any time. After a third week the swelling decreases and the period is over for about six months.

If you have an absolutely climb-proof and dig-proof run, within your yard, it will be safe to leave her there, but otherwise the female in season should be shut indoors. Don't leave her out alone for even a minute; she should be exercised only on leash. If you want to prevent the neighborhood dogs from hanging around your doorstep, as they inevitably will as soon as they discover that your female is in season, take her some distance away from the house before you let her relieve herself. Take her to a nearby park or field in the car for a chance to stretch her legs. After the three weeks are up you can let her out as before, with no worry that she can have puppies until the next season. But if you want to have her spayed, consult your veterinarian about the time and age at which he prefers to do it. With a young dog the operation is simple and after a night or two at the animal hospital she can be at home, wearing only a small bandage as a souvenir.

VETERINARY CARE

You will want your puppy to be protected against the most serious puppyhood diseases: distemper and infectious hepatitis. So your first action after getting him will be to take him to your veterinarian for his shots and a check-up, if he has not already received them. He may have had all or part of the immunization as early as two months, so check with the seller before you bring your puppy home.

You may give the puppy temporary serum which provides immunity for about two weeks, but nowadays permanent vaccine providing lifelong immunity can be given so early that the serum is seldom used, except as a precaution in outbreaks. The new vaccine is a combined one against distemper and hepatitis, and may be given in one or three (two weeks apart) shots. Your veterinarian probably has a preferred type, so go along with him, as either method is protective in a very high percentage of cases.

There is now an effective anti-rabies vaccine, which you can give to your dog if there should be an outbreak of this disease in your neighborhood. It is not permanent, however, so unless local regulations demand it, there is little value in giving the vaccine in ordinary circumstances.

WORMING

Your puppy has probably been wormed at least once, since puppies have a way of picking up worms, particularly in a kennel where they are exposed to other dogs. Find out when he was last wormed and the date, if any, for re-worming. Older dogs are usually able to throw off worms if they are in good condition when infected, but unless the puppy is given some help when he gets worms, he is likely to become seriously sick. New worm medicines containing the non-toxic but effective piperazines may be bought at your pet store or druggist's, and you can give them yourself. But remember to follow instructions carefully and do not worm the puppy unless you are sure he has worms.

If the puppy passes a long, string-like white worm in his stool or coughs one up, that is sufficient evidence, and you should proceed to worm him. Other indications are: general listlessness, a large belly, dull coat, mattery eye and coughing, but these could also be signs that your puppy is coming down with some disease. If you only *suspect* that he has worms, take him to your veterinarian for a check-up and stool examination before worming.

4. Caring for Your Adult German Shepherd

When your dog reaches his first birthday he is no longer a puppy, although he will not be fully mature and developed until he is two. For all intents and purposes, however, he may be considered full-grown and adult, now.

DIET

You may prefer to continue feeding your dog twice a day, although he can now eat all that he needs to be healthy at one meal a day. Usually it is best to feed that one meal, or the main meal, in the evening. Most dogs eat better this way, and digest their food better. If your dog skips an occasional meal, don't worry; after half an hour remove the food if he turns up his nose at it. Otherwise he will develop the habit of picking at his food, and food left out too long becomes stale or spoiled. If you use the dry self-feeding method, of course this does not apply.

The best indication of the correct amount to feed your dog is his state of health. A fat dog is not a healthy one; just like a fat person, he has to strain his heart—and his whole body—to carry excess weight. If you cannot give your dog more exercise, cut down on his food, and remember that those dog biscuits fed as snacks or rewards count in the calories. If your dog is thin, increase the amount and add a little more fat. You can also add flavoring he likes to pep up his appetite. The average grown dog needs 5 to 6 cups of dog meal, or a pound of canned food with an additional two cups of meal, per day. Use your own judgment for YOUR dog.

CLEANLINESS AND GROOMING

The Shepherd, with his clean ways and short coat, needs little in the way of grooming. From puppyhood he should be accustomed to brushing with a hound glove or stiff brush, and to having his teeth checked and being handled all over.

Your pet, like all outdoor dogs, does most of his shedding in spring and fall, although a dog which spends much of his time in the warm house will shed a little all year around. A vigorous brushing with a fairly stiff brush every day or two will prevent loose hair from becoming a nuisance. If your dog is accustomed to it as a puppy he will enjoy his grooming.

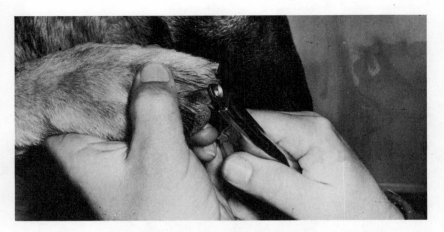

Use a special dog nail clipper to cut your German Shepherd's toenails. Be careful not to cut the fine vein which runs through the nail.

Teach him to jump onto a chest or large box, and to stay there while you brush him, cut his nails, or give him an inspection.

The toenails should be kept short, to prevent spreading the foot or the chance of their tearing and hurting him. A weekly clipping with specially designed clippers, available at your pet shop or department, will keep them under control. Never take off too much at one time, as you might cut the "quick" which is sensitive and will bleed as yours would. A sharp cut across the end, then the rounding off of the sides with a little clip, or a file, will keep them trim and help make the quick recede. Be particularly careful with black nails, in which the quick is not visible.

Your dog will seldom need a bath unless he gets into something smelly, or is unusually dirty. Too much bathing will dry the skin and cause shedding, so don't overdo it in any event. If you use soap be sure to rinse it all out so that the residue won't irritate his skin. He should be dried off and kept in a warm place afterward, so he won't be chilled.

If your dog's skin is dry or he sheds more than a little bit in spring and fall, it may be due to lack of fat in the diet. Rub a little olive oil into his coat and add a spoonful of lard to his food. Other skin troubles, shown by scratching, redness, or a sore on the surface, should be examined by your veterinarian, who can prescribe treatment and clear up the trouble quickly. Don't delay, as once it takes hold any skin disease is hard to cure.

NOSE, TEETH, EARS AND EYES

Normally a dog's nose, teeth, ears and eyes need no special care. The dog's nose is cool and moist to the touch (unless he has been in a warm house); however, the "cold nose" theory is only a partial indication of health

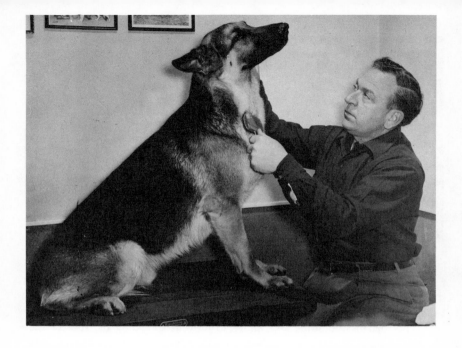

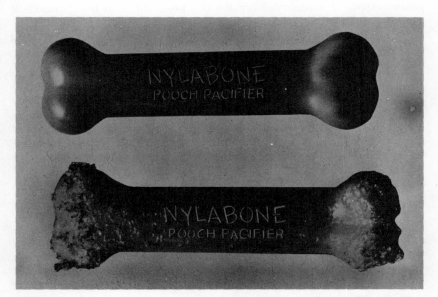

NYLABONE® is a necessity that is available at your local petshop (not in supermarkets). The puppy or grown dog chews the hambone flavored nylon into a frilly dog toothbrush, massaging his gums and cleaning his teeth as he plays. Veterinarians highly recommend this product . . . but beware of cheap imitations which might splinter or break.

or sickness. A fever, for instance, would be shown by a hot, dry nose, but other illness might not cause this. The dog's eyes are normally bright and alert, with the eyelid down in the corner, not over the eye. If the haw is bloodshot or partially covers the eye, it may be a sign of illness, or irritation. If your dog has matter in the corners of the eyes, bathe with a mild eye wash; obtain ointment from your veterinarian or pet shop to treat a chronic condition.

If your dog seems to have something wrong with his ears which causes him to scratch at them or shake his head, cautiously probe the ear with a cotton swab. An accumulation of wax will probably work itself out. But dirt or dried blood is indicative of ear mites or infection, and should be treated immediately. Sore ears in the summer, due to fly bites, should be

(Top, left page) A German Shepherd must be groomed regularly if he is to look healthy and well cared for. It is your duty to groom your dog properly.

(Bottom, left page) Special dog brushes are available to assist you in grooming your German Shepherd properly.

washed with mild soap and water, then covered with a soothing ointment, gauze-wrapped if necessary. Keep the dog protected from insects, inside if necessary, until his ears heal.

The dog's teeth will take care of themselves, although you may want your veterinarian to scrape off the unsightly tartar accumulation occasionally. A good hard bone will help to do the same thing.

PARASITES

Should your dog pick up fleas or other skin parasites from neighbors' dogs or from the ground, weekly use of a good DDT- or Chlordane-base flea powder will keep them off. Remember to dust his bed and change the bedding, too, as flea eggs drop off the host to hatch and wait in likely places for the dog to return. In warm weather a weekly dusting or monthly dip is good prevention.

If your grown dog is well fed and in good health you will probably have no trouble with worms. He may pick them up from other dogs, however, so if you suspect worms, have a stool examination made and, if necessary, worm him. Fleas, too, are carriers of tapeworm, so that is one good reason to make sure the dog is free from these insects. Roundworms, the dog's most common intestinal parasite, have a life cycle which permits complete eradication by worming twice, ten days apart. The first worming will remove all adults and the second will destroy all subsequently hatched eggs before they in turn can produce more parasites.

THE OLD DOG

With the increased knowledge and care available, there is no reason why your dog should not live to a good old age. As he grows older he may need a little additional care, however. Remember that a fat dog is not healthy, particularly as he grows older, and limit his food accordingly. The older dog needs exercise as much as ever, although his heart cannot bear the strain of sudden and violent exertion. His digestion may not be as good as it was as a puppy, so follow your veterinarian's advice about special feeding, if necessary. Failing eyesight or hearing mean lessened awareness of dangers, so you must protect him more than before. The old dog is used to his home, and to set ways, so too many strangers are bound to be a strain. For the same reason, boarding him out or a trip to the vet's are to be avoided unless absolutely necessary.

Should you decide at this time to get a puppy, to avoid being without a dog when your old retainer is no longer with you, be very careful how you introduce the puppy. He is naturally playful and will expect the older dog to respond to his advances. Sometimes the old dog will get a new lease on life from a pup. But don't make him jealous by giving to the newcomer the attention that formerly was exclusively his. Feed them apart, and show

This German Shepherd will make a fine pet, but he does not have a perfect face. His ear has a kink in it and though this does not affect his personality, it would cramp his style in the show ring! This type of malformation can disqualify a dog from the show.

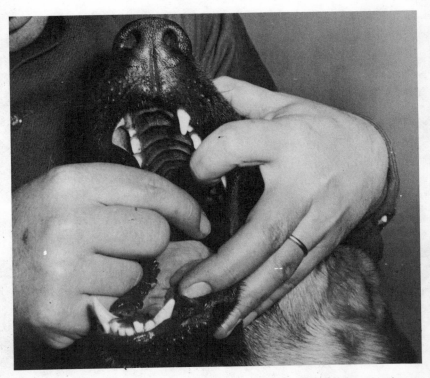

When giving your German Shepherd medicine, put the pill as far down his throat as you can and then shove it further in with your finger until he cannot spit it out.

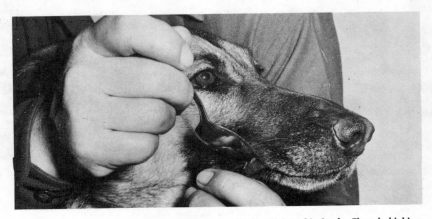

When giving liquid medicine, merely pour the liquid into his jowls. Then hold his head up so it will slip down into his throat and he will swallow it without losing any.

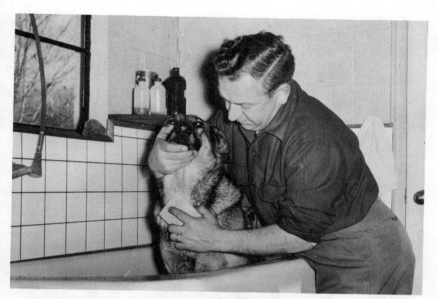

(Above) Be careful when you give your German Shepherd his occasional bath. Protect his eyes, nose and mouth from irritating soap.

(Below) Dry your dog off thoroughly before you allow him to roam about. A wet dog is highly sensitive to cold and drafts.

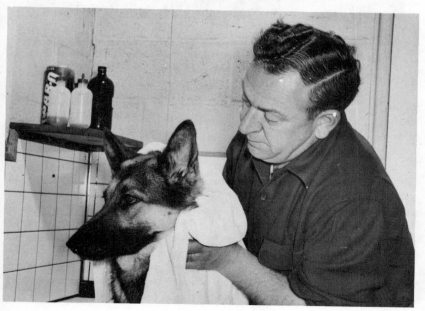

Not only can a German Shepherd be trained to guard your home, but he will also protect your children or act as a companion for the lonely child. There is so much truth to the saying, "A man's best friend is his dog!"

the old dog that you still love him the most; the puppy, not being used to individual attention will not mind sharing your love.

FIRST AID

Should your dog be injured, you can give him first aid which is, in general, similar to that for a human. The same principles apply. Superficial wounds should be disinfected and healing ointment applied. If the cut is likely to get dirty apply a bandage and restrain the dog so that he won't keep trying to remove it. A cardboard ruff will prevent him from licking his chest or body. Nails can be taped down to prevent scratching.

A board splint should be put on before moving a dog which might have a broken bone. If you are afraid that the dog will bite from pain, use a bandage muzzle made from a long strip of cloth, wrapped around the

Fully alert, ears held high, this magnificent German Shepherd is challenging a stranger approaching his domain.

muzzle, then tied under the jaw and brought up behind the ears to hold it on. In case of severe bleeding apply a tourniquet—a strip of cloth wrapped around a stick to tighten it will do—between the cut on a limb and the heart, but loosen it every few minutes to avoid damaging the circulation.

If you suspect that your dog has swallowed poison, try to get him to vomit by giving him salt water or mustard in water. In all these cases, rush him to your veterinarian as soon as possible, after alerting him by phone.

In warm weather the most important thing to remember for your dog's sake is providing fresh water. If he tends to slobber and drink too much, it may be offered at intervals of an hour or so instead of being available at all times, but it should be fresh and cool. Don't over-exercise the dog or let the children play too wildly with him in the heat of the day. Don't leave him outside without shade, and never leave a dog in a car which could become overheated in the sun. It should always have some shade and ventilation through the windows.

5. How to Train Your German Shepherd

ANIMAL OR PET?

There is only a one-word difference between an *animal* and a *pet* and that word is TRAINING.

But training your dog depends upon many factors:

how intelligent you are;

how intelligent the dog is;

what your intentions are;

how much time you are willing to devote to the task.

First we consider the dog owner who is merely interested in training his dog to be a perfect home companion, a dog that he can be proud to own, a dog that won't embarrass him by untimely "accidents" nor kill himself by running into the street.

THE DOG OWNER'S PART

Before you begin training your dog to be a pet, there are certain important facts to remember:

You are a human being and do not speak the same language that a dog does. So you must try to think as a pet dog thinks; your dog will try to understand his trainer.

Training your dog is like training a child. It requires firmness tempered with kindness, strictness but gentleness, consistency, repetition and above all PATIENCE. You must have the patience to go over the training cycle time and time again until the message reaches your dog.

Did you know that a dog is the only known animal that can be bribed into learning by just a few kind words and soft pats on the back? Other animals must be bribed with food or be beaten into submission, but not your pet dog. He wants kindness and attention. Reward him with a pat on the back when he is doing well and you will soon have a dog eager to learn.

GIVING COMMANDS

When you give commands use the shortest phrase possible and use the same word with the same meaning at all times. If you want to teach your dog to sit, then always use the word SIT. If you want your dog to lie down, then always use the word DOWN. It doesn't matter what word you use as long as your dog becomes accustomed to hearing it and acts upon it.

The trick hound dog that always sits on the command UP and stands on the command SIT was easily trained to understand the words that way. The words are merely sounds to him. He cannot understand you but he understands the tone of your voice and the inflection of the words.

Unless you are consistent in your use of commands you can never train your animal properly.

WHAT YOU WILL TEACH YOUR DOG

Your house pet should certainly learn the rudiments necessary to good behavior. Your dog should be housebroken first of all. Then he should learn how to walk properly with a collar and leash, after which he should be taught the simple commands of HEEL, SIT, COME and STAY. Only after the dog has learned these commands is it safe to train him off the leash.

Once your dog gets into the swing of his training it is wise to continue to train him in more difficult performances. After all, the hardest part of the job is establishing a communication system so that each of you learns what to expect from the other. Once your dog learns a trick or a command he will hardly ever forget it if you repeat it every so often. Begging, giving his paw, playing dead and rolling over, are entertaining tricks which you, your friends and your dog can all enjoy to mutual benefit. There are, however, more important lessons first.

COLLAR AND LEASH

As soon as you purchase your dog be sure that you stop at your pet shop and pick out the type of collar and leash that best suits your purposes. Leashes are available in many different colors and materials. You can buy a chain leash, a light plastic leash for small breed dogs, or a genuine leather leash for longer, more beautiful wear.

When buying your leash and collar be prepared to order the size you need. If you don't have a tape measure to gauge the collar size of your dog, merely take a piece of string and tie it loosely around your dog's neck. Mark off the distance and take this in with you so your salesman can give you the proper size.

If you decide on a collar for a puppy, buy one that fits nicely when on the tightest hole so that as your dog grows he can grow into the collar. If your dog is older, get one with a fit that takes the collar to the center hole so that fluctuations in his coat can be compensated for with a hole on either side. Collars and harnesses are made to last a long time, so be certain that you get one that your dog will not grow out of.

Once you have the proper size collar (or harness) for your puppy let him sniff it and play with it for a minute or two to get accustomed to the

Getting your dog to lie down, walk and sit is a simple matter, but it requires practice and patience. The hand signal, leash and collar and verbal commands are all you need. (Above) The trainer uses a right hand signal and says DOWN. (Top, right page) After walking, this German Shepherd has sighted an enemy and the trainer has shifted the leash to his left hand and shortened up. (Bottom, right page) As soon as the master stops walking and puts his feet together, the well-trained German Shepherd sits down.

smell of the material. Then gently hold the pup in your arms and slowly put the collar on him. Chances are that he won't like this strange feeling a bit, but don't give in. Just comfort him and play with him for a while and he'll forget all about it. Keep the collar on the dog at all times thereafter, except of course, when you bathe him.

WHAT ABOUT LESSONS?

Try to make your training lessons interesting and appealing both to yourself and your dog. Short frequent lessons are of much more value than long lessons. It is much better for all concerned if you teach your dog for 10 minutes at a time, three times a day, than for 30 minutes once a day. The 10 minute session amuses both you and your dog and the attachment which develops between you during these lessons will be everlasting.

A good time to train your dog is for 10 minutes before you give him his breakfast; then he assumes that the meal is a reward for his being such a good dog. If you follow this schedule for all three meals your training program will be extremely successful.

TRAINING YOUR DOG TO WALK PROPERLY

After your dog has been housebroken and has become accustomed to his collar or harness you must teach him to walk properly on a leash. We are assuming that you will use the collar and leash when housebreaking your puppy. Once he is thoroughly familiar with the workings of these restraining objects, you must teach him to respect the master at the other end of the leash.

You should hold the leash firmly in your right hand. The dog should walk on your left side with the leash crossing the front of your body. The reason for this will be obvious once you've actually walked your dog . . . you have more control this way.

Let your dog lead you for the first few moments so that he fully understands that freedom can be his if he goes about it properly. He knows already that when he wants to go outdoors the leash and collar are necessary, so he has respect for the leash. Now, if while walking, he starts to pull in one direction all you do is *stop walking*. He will walk a few steps and then find that he can't walk any further. He will then turn and look into your face. *This is the crucial point.* Just stand there for a moment and stare right back at him . . . Now walk another ten feet and stop again. Again your dog will probably walk out the leash, find he can't go any further, and turn around and look again. If he starts to pull and jerk then just stand there. After he quiets down, just bend down and comfort him as he may be frightened. Keep up this training until he learns not to outwalk you.

You must understand that most dogs like to stop and sniff around a bit until they find THE place to do their duty. Be kind enough to stop and wait when they find it necessary to pause. This is the whole story . . . it's as easy as that. A smart dog can learn to walk properly in a few days, provided you have taught him correctly from the beginning. A dog that is incorrectly trained initially may take a month to retrain, but in any event, every dog can learn to walk properly on a leash!

TRAINING YOUR DOG TO COME TO YOU

Your dog has been named and he knows his name. After hearing his name called over and over again in your home, he finds that it pays to come when called. Why? Because you only call him when his food is ready or when you wish to play with him and pet him. Outside the house it is a different story. He would rather play by himself or with other dogs or chase a cat than play with you. So, he must be trained to come to you when he is called. Here's how to do it:

After you have trained your pet to walk properly on a leash let him walk out the entire length of the leash. Then stop and call him to you. If he just stands there looking up with those soulful eyes that made you buy him in the first place, then gently pull on the leash until he comes to your feet, even if you have to drag him over. By no means should you walk to him! If you have some "candy" for dogs, which you can get at your pet shop, give him one after you've pulled him to you. Pat his head, making a big fuss over him as though you haven't seen him for weeks!

Then walk along and try it all over again. Repeat the process until he finally gets the idea. It shouldn't take long if you are consistent about it every time you take him out for his walk. Don't forget the dog candy because if you get him to learn that a satisfactory performance earns him a piece, the more difficult lessons will be easier to get across.

TRAINING YOUR DOG TO STAY AT YOUR SIDE

From here on, the training gets a bit more difficult. So far the house-breaking, walking and coming when called has constituted the basic training EVERY dog must know. What follows is more difficult to teach and is harder for the dog to learn because it means he has to give up some of his freedom and playfulness.

To train your dog to stay by your side is a little harder than to train him not to pull on the leash. For the "heel training" you must get another type collar — *a choke chain collar*. It is made of polished, chrome chain and it is designed to tighten about your dog's neck if he pulls too hard. The collar is definitely not a cruel instrument (as the name might imply). Here's what you do:

Put the choke chain collar on your dog the next time you take him out. If he pulls too hard, this type collar will definitely break that habit one, two, three! Once you've gotten him accustomed to the action of the choke chain collar stop the walk and start out again with the dog's nose even with your left knee. Walk quickly, repeating as you go the word HEEL over and over

A German Shepherd has a magnificent coat. Keep it healthy by proper grooming!

again. If your dog walks out past your knee, jerk him back firmly, but not *cruelly,* raising your voice HEEL at the same time. If he persists in going out in front of you all the time, stop and start all over again. Repeat this process until he learns it . . . Have patience, for once he learns to walk by your side in this manner, you will have a well-mannered dog all his life.

Some dogs are a bit lazy and will walk behind you instead of in front of you. If your dog does this, stop and call him to you and keep calling him with the word HEEL until he finally gets the idea. After each proper performance offer him some dog candy. Keep your dog informed that the word HEEL means he is to walk close to your left heel.

After your dog has learned to HEEL on a tight lead, you can use a slack leash and let him wear his normal, everyday collar. If he forgets himself, put the choke chain collar on again right away. Don't give him a chance to forget his lessons . . . and don't forget to use the same word HEEL at all times.

In training the German Shepherd for police and war work, special trainers are utilized to pose as "criminals" or "enemies." Dogs thus trained are not pets, but working animals.

TRAINING YOUR DOG TO STOP WITHOUT COMMAND

When your dog has been trained to HEEL on a loose leash, the next step in his training is to STOP without command so that if you stop for a street corner or to talk to someone along the way, your dog doesn't pull you to get going. Training to stop without command requires use of the choke chain collar for the first lessons.

Take your dog out for his usual walk, keeping him at HEEL all the time. Then stop dead in your tracks keeping the leash tight in your hands without a bit of slack. DO NOT LET HIM SIT DOWN! No command is necessary.

As soon as he stops, pat him on the back and give him some dog candy. Then walk on again briskly and stop short. Keep your dog on the tight leash at all times and repeat this until he learns that he must stop dead in his tracks just as you do. When you stop, stop *deliberately* so that he can actually anticipate your stopping and be with you at all times. You can tell when he is being attentive for he will walk a few steps and then turn his head so that he can keep an eye on your face. He will actually crave to satisfy you once he has been properly taught, and he will only take a few steps before he swings his head to look at you. Next time you see a well-trained dog walking along the street, notice how much time he spends looking at his master instead of at other things.

Once your dog has learned to stop without command and you want to walk again, you can signal him by many means. One way is to slacken your leash and then start walking so that he will learn that a slackened leash means you intend to walk again. Another way is to signal him verbally with the word "Go" or "Come on Pal" or something similar to that. It doesn't matter what word you use as long as you use the same word all the time.

OFF-THE-LEASH TRAINING

After your dog has accomplished these lessons it is time to begin his training without a leash. Try to find a large open area which is fenced in. It will be safer to advance to this stage within the confines of that area. If no such area is available, find as quiet a street as you can (even late at night so that few automobiles are around) and begin your training there.

Let's assume that your dog heels and stops without command. After you've walked him a few feet and tested him on stopping without command, bend down and remove the leash. Start walking briskly as you did when training him to heel. Stop suddenly without command and see if he does the same. If he doesn't, then immediately snap on the leash with the choke collar and go through the training again. Walk once with the leash on and once with the leash off, until finally your dog gets the idea that he can have more freedom by behaving himself, than misbehaving. Don't forget to carry some dog candy along with you so you can reward him for a successful performance.

It is important for you and your dog to use his regular collar during "off-training" hours, since your dog likes a recess every few days. Then when you put on the training collar he knows that something new is coming along. Every time you put on the training collar give him a piece of candy and an extra pat or two. Let him know that both of you are going to enjoy the new experience.

TEACHING YOUR DOG TO SIT

Once your dog has mastered the art of heeling with a regular collar, put on his choke chain collar and start a new lesson.

After a brisk walk go through the previous lessons as far as the short stop, your dog will be standing watching you and waiting for the loose leash to walk on further. When you reach this point, gently push his hind quarters down with your left hand as you hold the leash tightly raised in your right hand. This will keep his head up and his butt down. Don't let him lie all the way down or cower. Use just enough pressure so he knows to sit. Once he's in the sitting position give him a piece of dog candy, a few pats on the head and start walking again.

Do this several times. He should go into the sitting position every time you want him to, provided you let him know when you want him to sit.

Remember that when you stopped your dog was standing at your side ready to go off again whenever you were ready. Now use the word SIT very often so he can accustom his ears to *that* sound. Every time you push his hind-quarters down, say SIT. Keep repeating this word over and over again as you push him down. Soon he will learn when he should sit and when he should stay close to your side when you stop for a short time.

After thoroughly training your dog in sitting with a leash, go through the same method of training without a leash. A simple method is to walk along briskly, stop and tell him to SIT. As soon as he sits take the leash off and walk again. Then stop and tell him to SIT again.

If he doesn't sit upon command, hold his choke chain in your hand and force his hindquarters down into the sitting position. Do this again and again until he learns. As soon as he gets it right, give him a piece of dog candy. Repeat this training until it is thoroughly ingrained in his habits. It is always important to keep in mind that you must never start a new lesson until the old one is mastered. Inconsistency on your part is considered a weakness by your dog.

TRAINING YOUR DOG TO LIE DOWN

Now that your dog can sit with a leash or without a leash and is thoroughly familiar with your training routine, perhaps you want to train him to lie down. Many people feel that there is no reason for teaching him to lie down and they don't bother, but if you want him to ride safely in an automobile, training in lying down is important.

Usually DOWN is the command word for lying down although any word you use will be acceptable, provided you use the same word to have the same meaning every time you use it.

Take your dog out and go through the training sequence until you have him in a sitting position. Then walk in front of him and gently pull his two front paws forward so that he automatically falls into the lying down position. As you do this say DOWN. If he raises his hindquarters then use the command SIT and his hindquarters should drop immediately. Only constant repetition of this exercise will finally get him to lie down immediately upon command.

It is very helpful to use a hand signal along with the verbal command

This German Shepherd is in the "stay" position, alertly awaiting further commands from his master.

DOWN. The usual hand signal is to extend your left hand, with your palm down, as a sign to lie down. A very successful variation is merely to point down as you give the order. Any signal is satisfactory as long as you are consistent.

When giving the hand signal be careful that your dog doesn't think you are threatening him. You can dispel this fear by immediately offering him some dog candy each time he successfully completes the lying down maneuver.

TEACHING YOUR DOG TO STAY

The main objective in teaching your dog to sit and lie down is to get him to stay where you want him. Many times you will restrict him to a certain room, possibly the kitchen. When the front door rings, you don't want him tracking through the house. Will you have to lock him in the kitchen before you open the front door? Do you want him to follow you all over the house whenever you move from room to room? If the answer to these questions is to be "No!," then he must be trained to stay.

Then again, what more beautiful sight is there than to see a dog "parked" outside a supermarket (while his master is buying dog candy!) waiting in a sitting or lying down position. No one but his master's command can budge him. Though strangers may pat him and entice him, nothing can make him move from the position he is in. These are some of the rewards you receive by training.

To train your dog to stay is not a difficult feat at all. Once he sits or lies upon command, proceed with the STAY command. Immediately after he is seated (or lying down) drop the leash and walk away three or four steps. Keep facing him while you are doing this, and, if he starts to rise to follow you, raise your voice and give the hand signal DOWN! If he doesn't get down immediately, walk back to him very briskly and force him down in no uncertain manner. Then try again to walk a few feet from him. Repeat this sequence until he finally stays at the command. The following day walk a little bit further; keep up this training until finally you can walk away, out of sight, and he will stay where he is, waiting for you.

When you want your dog to rise out of the position he is in, command COME (or call his name, whichever way you have decided earlier in his training). Do not allow him to run to you from the STAY position because you return to his line of vision. He must await your permission to come to you. This part of the training either makes or breaks a dog. The test is simple for an obedient, well disciplined dog. If you are lax and inconsistent in the initial stages, then it will be impossible to train him to stay.

DISCIPLINE TRAINING FOR YOUR DOG

Up to this point you have been training your dog to act upon command. Now you will attempt to train his intelligence. This is another important part of the training problem and it is the part that separates a "smart" dog from one that doesn't "use his head."

All dogs, regardless of their training, will get the urge to run after another dog, to chase a cat, to fetch, or just to run for the sheer love of running. In the open field or park this is perfectly all right, but in the city it can be catastrophic! Let's assume that your dog has a bad habit of slipping off his collar and making a mad dash away from you. You may find this out some fine, bright morning when both of you are in fine spirits: He will spot a cat, and without warning will dash off, either pulling the leash right out of your unwary hands or slipping his head out of the collar. A moment of panic will hit you both. But, once the initial impact of the moment is over, he will come scampering back at the command COME.

At this point do not beat your dog. He knows he has done something wrong and he is a bit confused himself. Just pat him on the head and ignore it . . . *this time.* Then walk back to the house and get a long rope, 25 to 30 feet long. Tie this rope to his regular collar (do not use a choke chain) and also use the regular leash. Try to get your dog into the same situation as the one he bolted from. When he runs away from you again (if he does), drop the leash but hold onto the rope. When he gets far enough away give a loud holler STOP and jerk the rope at the same time. He will spin in his tracks and lay where he is, thoroughly confused and a bit scared.

Go over to him and make a big fuss over him as though you can't imagine what happened. Tell him he should never have left your side. Repeat this training four or five times and he will never bolt from you again.

You can practice the command STOP by running a few steps with him and then shouting the command STOP as you suddenly stop short. By repeating the command STOP in every such situation it won't be too long before you can make your dog STOP on a dime!

KEEPING YOUR DOG OFF THE FURNITURE

Your favorite sofa or chair will also be your dog's favorite seat. It is naturally used the most and so will have the odors (which only your dog can smell) of the beloved master. There are two ways of training your dog out of the habit of sitting in your chair. (You will want to break the habit because most dogs shed and their hair gets all over your clothes. Then again, he might like to curl up in your lap while you are trying to read or knit.)

The simplest way of breaking the habit is to soak a small rag with a special dog scent which is repulsive to dogs. Put the rag on the chair which your dog favors. He will jump on the chair, get a whiff of the scent and make a detour of the chair forever more!

Another way to train is to pull him off the chair every time you catch him there and immediately command him to lie DOWN at your feet. Then give him a severe tongue lashing. After a few times he will never go to the chair again WHILE YOU ARE AROUND! The greater problem is to teach him to stay away all the time. The usual plan is to get a few inexpensive

German Shepherds will try to get away with as much as you will let them. Train them to stay off your furniture, or your guests will be walking home with dog hair all over their clothes.

mouse traps and set them (without bait of course) with a few sheets of newspaper over them. As soon as your dog jumps onto the chair the mouse-trap goes SNAP and off the chair goes the dog. He may try it again, but then the second trap will go off, and he will have learned his lesson.

Since your dog has his own bed, train him to stay in it when you don't want him to be any place else. This can be done by saying the word BED in a loud voice and dragging him over and placing him in it. Do this a few times and he will learn where to go when you want him in bed!

TRAINING YOUR DOG NOT TO BARK

For people who live close to another family, a barking dog is a nuisance and your dog must be trained not to bark unless he hears a very strange sound or sees a stranger on your premises. Do not forget that barking is to a dog what a voice is to a human and he expresses happiness, alarm, pain and warning in his bark. It would be impossible to write down all the different sounds that a dog can make, but you will recognize the difference between a whimper, a growl, a howl and a bark. A whimper denotes pain

Don't fool around with the training of your dog. A German Shepherd is one of the most intelligent members of dogdom, and once he has learned to hate a person, that person will never be safe around the dog again.

or discomfort. A growl denotes danger and is a warning. A howl denotes loneliness and a bark denotes strange sounds.

To break your dog of excess barking merely requires the use of a rolled newspaper. Every time he barks for some unknown reason, or barks excessively when strangers approach, swat your own hand smartly with the rolled paper, making as loud a smack as possible and at the same time command QUIET. This has never failed to stop a dog. You must repeat this every time he howls.

Certain dogs, regardless of training or breeding, howl and bark all night long and nothing short of chloroform can stop them.

TRAINING YOUR DOG NOT TO JUMP ON PEOPLE

Some dogs are so affectionate that they will jump on everybody who comes into sight in order to get their attention and affection. Only you can train your dog not to jump and it's an easy trick to learn. As he jumps up to greet *you*, merely bend your knee so he hits it with his chest and falls over. He cannot see your knee coming up as his head will be above your knee. After a few falls he will get the idea that it isn't practical to jump up to greet you or anyone.

Of course if he has learned the meaning of the command DOWN, then use that command when he jumps up. He won't like to assume the down position when he is anxious for a pat or piece of dog candy, so this will be an easy lesson for him to learn.

TRAINING YOUR DOG TO DO TRICKS

Nearly every housedog learns a few tricks without training during the course of his puppyhood. These are usually accidentally learned, but the

This German Shepherd has been trained to protect the car in which his master leaves the shopping items. Salesmen who must make frequent stops find that it is of tremendous help to have a "police dog" along. It not only promotes his product when people stop to admire the dog, but it saves him a lot of time in locking and unlocking his car at each stop.

You must train your German Shepherd to stay away from moving cars. A car-chasing dog sooner or later comes to grief.

master observes the dog doing them and then prompts him to repeat the same thing over and over again.

You will deliberately want to train your dog to shake hands. First get him into the sitting position. Then upon the command PAW, lift his paw in your hand and shake it vigorously without knocking him off balance. Then give him a piece of dog candy. Repeat this several times a day and in a week he will all but hold out his paw when you walk in the door!

Teaching your dog to beg is done in the same manner. Place him in the sitting position with the proper command. Then lift his front paws up until he is in a begging position. Hold him that way until he finds a comfortable balance and then let him balance himself. As he gets his balance, hold a piece of dog candy right over his nose. As soon as you let go of his front paws, lower the dog candy to his mouth and let him take it from your hands. Hold the dog candy firmly so it takes a few seconds for him to pry it loose, during this time you are saying BEG, over and over. From then on, you must bribe him with dog candy until he assumes the begging position upon the command BEG. Repeat the preliminary training until he eagerly goes into the begging position to earn dog candy.

TRAINING YOUR DOG TO RETRIEVE

Most dogs are born retrievers and their natural instinct is to chase something that moves. First go to a pet shop and pick out a rubber toy. Try a rubber ball, a rubber bone, anything that attracts your eye. They are all made of completely harmless rubber and are safe even if your dog chews them up.

Then take your dog outside and throw the toy a few feet. He will usually chase it and pick it up. If he doesn't, then you must walk him over to the toy and place it in his mouth and walk him back to your starting position with it. Repeat this operation until he learns the game. Once he goes after the toy, call him to you. If he drops it along the way merely send him back for it by pointing to the object. If necessary, walk him back to the toy, put it in his mouth and walk back with him to the original starting position. When he successfully brings back the object you can reward him with a piece of dog candy.

6. Caring for the Female and Raising Puppies

Whether or not you bought your female dog intending to breed her, some preparation is necessary when and if you decide to take this step.

WHEN TO BREED

It is usually best to breed on the second or third season. Plan in advance the time of year which is best for you, taking into account where the puppies will be born and raised. You will keep them until they are at least six weeks old, and a litter of husky pups takes up considerable space by then. Other considerations are selling the puppies (Christmas vs. springtime sales), your own vacation, and time available to care for them. You'll need at least an hour a day to feed and clean up after the mother and puppies but probably it will take you much longer—with time out to admire and play with them!

CHOOSING THE STUD

You can plan to breed your female about 6½ months after the start of her last season, although a variation of a month or two either way is not unusual. Choose the stud dog and make arrangements well in advance. If you are breeding for show stock, which may command better prices, a mate should be chosen with an eye to complementing the deficiencies of your female. If possible, they should have several ancestors in common within the last two or three generations, as such combinations generally "click" best. He should have a good show record or be the sire of show winners if old enough to be proven.

The owner of such a male usually charges a fee for the use of the dog of $50 or more. This does not guarantee a litter, but you generally have the right to breed your female again if she does not have puppies. In some cases the owner of the stud will agree to take a choice puppy in place of a stud fee. You should settle all details beforehand, including the possibility of a single surviving puppy, deciding the age at which he is to make his choice and take the pup, and so on.

If you want to raise a litter "just for the fun of it" and plan merely to make use of an available male, the most important selection point is temperament. Make sure the dog is friendly as well as healthy, because a bad disposition could appear in his puppies, and this is the worst of all traits in a dog destined to be a pet. In such cases a "stud fee puppy," not necessarily the choice of the litter, is the usual payment.

PREPARATION FOR BREEDING

Before you breed your female, make sure she is in good health. She should be neither too thin nor too fat. Any skin disease *must* be cured, before it can be passed on to the puppies. If she has worms she should be wormed before being bred or within three weeks afterward. It is generally considered a good idea to revaccinate her against distemper and hepatitis before the puppies are born. This will increase the immunity the puppies receive during their early, most vulnerable period.

The female will probably be ready to breed 12 days after the first colored discharge. You can usually make arrangements to board her with the owner of the male for a few days, to insure her being there at the proper time, or you can take her to be mated and bring her home the same day. If she still appears receptive she may be bred again two days later. However, some females never show signs of willingness, so it helps to have the experience of a breeder. Usually the second day after the discharge changes color is the proper time, and she may be bred for about three days following. For an additional week or so she may have some discharge and attract other dogs by her odor, but can seldom be bred.

THE FEMALE IN WHELP

You can expect the puppies nine weeks from the day of breeding, although 61 days is as common as 63. During this time the female should receive normal care and exercise. If she was overweight, don't increase her food at first; excess weight at whelping time is bad. If she is on the thin side build her up, giving some milk and biscuit at noon if she likes it. You may add one of the mineral and vitamin supplements to her food, to make sure that the puppies will be healthy. As her appetite increases, feed her more. During the last two weeks the puppies grow enormously and she will probably have little room for food and less appetite. She should be tempted with meat, liver and milk, however.

As the female in whelp grows heavier, cut out violent exercise and jumping. Although a dog used to such activities will often play with the children or run around voluntarily, restrain her for her own sake.

PREPARING FOR THE PUPPIES

Prepare a whelping box a few days before the puppies are due, and allow the mother to sleep there overnight or to spend some time in it during the day to become accustomed to it. Then she is less likely to try to have her pups under the front porch or in the middle of your bed. A variety of places will serve such as a corner of your cellar, garage, or an unused room. If the weather is warm, a large outdoor doghouse will do, well protected from rain or draft. A whelping box serves to separate mother and puppies from visitors and other distractions. The walls should be high enough to restrain the puppies, yet allow the mother to get away from the puppies after she has fed them. Four feet square is minimum size, and one-foot walls will keep the pups in until they begin to climb, when it should be built up. Then the puppies really need more room anyway, so double the space with a very low partition down the middle and you will find them naturally housebreaking themselves.

Layers of newspaper spread over the whole area will make excellent bedding and be absorbent enough to keep the surface warm and dry. They should be removed daily and replaced with another thick layer. An old quilt or washable blanket makes better footing for the nursing puppies than slippery newspaper during the first week, and is softer for the mother.

Be prepared for the actual whelping several days in advance. Usually the female will tear up papers, refuse food and generally act restless. These may be false alarms; the real test is her temperature, which will drop to below 100° about 12 hours before whelping. Take it with a rectal thermometer morning and evening, and put her in the pen, looking in on her frequently, when the temperature goes down.

WHELPING

Usually little help is needed but it is wise to stay close to make sure that the mother's lack of experience does not cause an unnecessary accident. Be ready to help when the first puppy arrives, for it could smother if she does not break the membrane enclosing it. She should start right away to lick the puppy, drying and stimulating it, but you can do it with a soft rough towel, instead. The afterbirth should follow the birth of each puppy, attached to the puppy by the long umbilical cord. Watch to make sure that each is expelled, anyway, for retaining this material can cause infection. In her instinct for cleanliness the mother will probably eat the afterbirth after biting the cord. One or two will not hurt her; they stimulate milk supply as well as labor for remaining pups. But too many can make her lose appetite for the food she needs to feed her pups and regain her strength. So remove the rest of them along with the wet newspapers and keep the pen dry and clean to relieve her anxiety.

If the mother does not bite the cord, or does it too close to the body, take over the job, to prevent an umbilical hernia. Tearing is recommended,

This German Shepherd had a litter of six puppies. As a rule German Shepherd bitches make wonderful mothers.

but you can cut it, about two inches from the body, with a sawing motion of scissors, sterilized in alcohol. Then dip the end in a shallow dish of iodine; the cord will dry up and fall off in a few days.

The puppies should follow each other at intervals of not more than half an hour. If more time goes past and you are sure there are still pups to come, a brisk walk outside may start labor again. If she is actively straining without producing a puppy it may be presented backward, a so-called "breach" or upside down birth. Careful assistance with a well-soaped finger to feel for the puppy or ease it back may help, but never attempt to pull it by force against the mother. This could cause serious damage, so let an expert handle it.

If anything seems wrong, waste no time in calling your veterinarian, who can examine her and if necessary give hormones which will bring the remaining puppies. You may want his experience in whelping the litter even if all goes well. He will probably prefer to have the puppies born at his hospital rather than to get up in the middle of the night to come to your home. The mother would, no doubt, prefer to stay at home, but you can be sure she will get the best of care in his hospital. If the puppies are born at home and all goes as it should, watch the mother carefully afterward.

It is not a bad idea to have the veterinarian check her and the pups. But most German Shepherds have little trouble, and usually, they know more about whelping than people, anyway.

WEANING THE PUPPIES

Hold each puppy to a breast as soon as he is dry, for a good meal without competition. Then he may join his littermates in the basket, out of his mother's way while she is whelping. Keep a supply of evaporated milk on hand for emergencies, or later weaning. A formula of evaporated milk, corn syrup and a little water with egg yolk should be warmed and fed in a doll or baby bottle if necessary. A supplementary feeding often helps weak pups over the hump. Keep track of birth weights, and weekly readings, thereafter; it will furnish an accurate record of the pups' growth and health.

After the puppies have arrived, take the mother outside for a walk and drink, and then leave her to take care of them. She will probably not want to stay away more than a minute or two for the first few weeks. Be sure to keep water available at all times, and feed her milk or broth frequently, as she needs liquids to produce milk. Encourage her to eat, with her favorite foods, until she asks for it of her own accord. She will soon develop a ravenous appetite and should have at least two large meals a day, with dry food available in addition.

Prepare a warm place to put the puppies after they are born to keep them dry and help them to a good start in life. An electric heating pad or hot water bottle covered with flannel in the bottom of a cardboard box should be set near the mother so that she can see her puppies. She will usually allow you to help, but don't take the puppies out of sight, and let her handle things if your interference seems to make her nervous.

Be sure that all the puppies are getting enough to eat. If the mother, sits or stands, instead of lying still to nurse, the probable cause is scratching from the puppies' nails. You can remedy this by clipping them, as you do hers. Manicure scissors will do for these tiny claws. Some breeders advise disposing of the smaller or weaker pups in a large litter, as the mother has trouble in handling more than six or seven. But you can help her out by preparing an extra puppy box or basket. Leave half the litter with the mother and the other half in a warm place, changing off at two hour intervals at first. Later you may change them less frequently, leaving them all together except during the day. Try supplementary feeding, too; as soon as their eyes open, at about two weeks, they will lap from a dish, anyway.

The puppies should normally be completely weaned at five weeks, although you start to feed them at three weeks. They will find it easier to lap semi-solid food than to drink milk at first, so mix baby cereal with whole or evaporated milk, warmed to body temperature, and offer it to the puppies in a saucer. Until they learn to lap it is best to feed one or two at a time, because they are more likely to walk into it than to eat. Hold the saucer at chin level, and let them gather around, keeping paws out of the dish. A damp sponge afterward prevents most of the cereal from sticking to the skin if the mother doesn't clean them up. Once they have gotten the idea, broth or babies' meat soup may be alternated with milk, and you can start them on finely chopped meat. At four weeks they will eat four meals a day, and soon do without their mother entirely. Start them on mixed dog food, or leave it with them in a dish for self-feeding. Don't leave water with them all the time; at this age everything is to play with and they will use it as a wading pool. They can drink all they need if it is offered several times a day, after meals.

As the puppies grow up the mother will go into the pen only to nurse them, first sitting up and then standing. To dry her up completely, keep the mother away for longer periods; after a few days of part-time nursing she can stay away for longer periods, and then completely. The little milk left will be resorbed.

AIRING THE PUPPIES

The puppies may be put outside, unless it is too cold, as soon as their eyes are open, and will benefit from the sunlight and vitamins. A rubber mat or newspapers underneath will protect them from cold or damp. At six weeks they can go outside permanently unless it is very cold, but make sure that they go into their shelter at night or in bad weather. By now cleaning up is a man-sized job, so put them out at least during the day and make your task easier. Be sure to clean their run daily, as worms and other infections are lurking. You can expect the pups to need at least one worming before they are ready to go to new homes, so take a stool sample to your veterinarian before they are three weeks old. If one puppy has worms all should be wormed. Follow the veterinarian's advice, and this applies also to vaccination. If you plan to keep a pup you will want to vaccinate him at the earliest age, so his littermates should be done at the same time.

7. Showing Your German Shepherd

As your puppy grows he will doubtless have many admirers among your friends, some of whom are bound to say, "Oh, what a handsome dog —you should certainly show him!" Perhaps even a breeder or judge will say he has show possibilities, and although you didn't buy him with that thought in mind, "Cinderella" champions do come along now and then— often enough to keep dog breeders perennially optimistic.

If you do have ideas of showing your dog, get the opinion of someone with experience first. With favorable criticism, go ahead making plans to show him. For the novice dog and handler, sanction shows are a good way to gain ring poise and experience. These are small shows often held by the local kennel club or breed specialty club, found in many cities. Entry fees are low and paid at the door, breeds and sexes are usually judged together, and the prizes and ribbons are not important. They provide a good opportunity to learn what goes on at a show, and to conquer ring nervousness. Matches are usually held during the evening or on a week-end afternoon, and you need stay only to be judged.

Before you go to a show your dog should be trained—to gait at a trot beside you, with head up and in a straight line. In the ring you will have to gait around the edge with other dogs and then individually up and down the center runner. In addition the dog must stand for examination by the judge, who will look at him closely and feel his head and body structure. He should be taught to stand squarely, hind feet slightly back, head up on the alert. He must hold the pose when you place his feet and show animation for a piece of boiled liver in your hand or a toy mouse thrown in front of you.

ADVANCE PREPARATION

Showing requires practice training sessions in advance; get a friend to act as judge and set the dog up and "show" him for a few minutes every day.

The day before the benched point show, pack your kit. You will want to take a water dish and bottle of water for your dog (so that he won't be

Don't allow your pet German Shepherd to bother you for food when you are eating. Scold him severely. He should be fed in his own area and kept out of your dining area when you eat.

affected by a change in drinking water, and you won't have to go look for it). A chain or leash to fasten him to the bench, or stall, where he must remain during the show, and a show lead should be included, as well as grooming tools. The show lead is a thin nylon or cord collar and leash combined, which detracts from the dog's appearance less than a clumsier chain and lead. Also put in the identification ticket sent by the show super-intendent, noting the time you must be there and place where the show will be held, as well as time of judging.

Don't feed your dog the morning of the show, or give him at most a light meal. He will be more comfortable in the car on the way, and will show more enthusiastically. When you arrive at the show grounds an official veterinarian will check your dog for health, and then you should find his bench and settle him there.